I0836123

MYRTLEFIELD
HOUSE

RUTH

MYRTLEFIELD
seeing the **BIG** picture

seeing the BIG picture helps readers grasp the rich sweep of each book of the Bible—what it says, why it was written and why it still matters today. Concise and engaging, each volume offers a clear view of the big themes and key truths that shape God's word. Whether you're discovering the Bible's message for the first time or teaching it to others, come and enjoy the big picture in a little frame.

Books in this series:

Ruth: How love's redeeming work is done
Titus: God's way of making beautiful people

RUTH

How love's **redeeming work** is done

DAVID GOODING

MYRTLEFIELD
seeing the **BIG** picture

RUTH: How love's redeeming work is done

This book was edited from David Gooding's sermons by Myrtlefield House editors. No generative artificial intelligence (AI) was used in the writing of this work.

Sometimes Dr Gooding gives his own translations or paraphrases.

Cover design: Ben Bredeweg
Cover image: James Tissot (1836–1902), 'Ruth Gleaning', modified
Typesetting: Peter F. Whyte

First published in English in 2026.

Published by The Myrtlefield Trust
PO BOX 2216, Belfast, BT1 9YR
w: www.myrtlefieldhouse.com
e: info@myrtlefieldhouse.com

ISBN: 978-1-83676-068-9 (pbk.)
ISBN: 978-1-83676-069-6 (PDF)
ISBN: 978-1-83676-070-2 (Kindle)
ISBN: 978-1-83676-071-9 (EPUB without DRM)

30 29 28 27 26 10 9 8 7 6 5 4 3 2 1

CONTENTS

INTRODUCTION

This is a magnificent story, rich in its various levels of meaning like a sophisticated tapestry with its many strands and patterns. It is the inspired revelation of God and part of his signature upon the pages of his word. Its richness speaks to our minds, even more so to our hearts and spirits. Here we find no insubstantial things. We hear them as the true sayings of God, and they cause our hope to rise up again and our spirits to rejoice. As we listen to his word and ponder these things, may God help us to glean from the wonders of his redemption, and the inexhaustible treasures of his almighty Son.

As Naomi did, let those of us who are older seek his grace to continue his work. And, like Ruth, may those of us who are younger seek to grow to become valiant men and women of God in this generation, carrying the torch of the great inheritance until the Lord comes and the final and glorious purposes of God are fully demonstrated before heaven and earth, for the glory of Jesus Christ our Lord.

Before you continue, take a little time to read the four short chapters of Ruth. Tap or scan the QR code to read online.

1

FROM DESOLATION TO RESTORATION

Readings: Ruth 1:1–22; 2:11–12; 3:5–10; 4:13–17

Before you continue, take a little time to read these passages from Ruth. Tap or scan the QR code to read online.

The book of Ruth is one of the best known and best loved books in the whole of the Old Testament. It is, in the first place, a delightful love story, and all the more delightful because of its purity. It is set historically in the time of Israel's judges, and the love story it presents stands in vivid contrast to the dark and lurid scenes at the end of the book of Judges. The contrast brings into focus the story of Ruth and Boaz as an appealing story of healthy human love and family life. There is also, of course, a romantic side to this ancient story, but we shall see that the marriage of Ruth and Boaz doesn't turn out to be quite so romantic as our modern sense of the term might suggest.

The fact is that the book is not primarily about Ruth. She and Boaz are certainly the key figures, for all the action of the book turns on them. The true subject matter of the book is introduced right at the start (1:1–6, 11–22). Then we have the conclusion to this wonderful story, the end to which all the action is designed and directed (4:13–17).

NAOMI'S STORY

So the book of Ruth is, strictly speaking, not about Ruth; it's about Naomi. You see that from the very beginning in how the story is introduced.

There was this man, Elimelech, who had a wife and two sons, and when a famine came in the land he went down and lived in the country of Moab. He died, says the narrative, moving very swiftly on without filling in any more details, concentrating at this stage on what the chief element in the story is. He died, and Naomi, his wife, was left without her husband. Meanwhile, their sons, Mahlon and Chilion, had married two young Moabite women, and then both sons also died, apparently childless. So now, says the historian, the woman was left without her two sons and her husband.

That is the initial point the story writer wants to make. The story is about a woman, now in middle life and perhaps beyond, who had had to uproot her home and go with her husband and their sons to Moab because of the famine that had come upon their village. She is trying to make a new life with her family in that foreign country when the first disaster strikes and she's left a widow. Then, to her horror, her two sons, who were childless, both die. Now she is completely desolate, left only with her daughters-in-law. What is she to do?

She hears news that the Lord has visited his people back in Bethlehem, giving them food. So she decides to uproot herself once more and return home. At the beginning, her daughters-in-law follow her, but then, with all realism, she tries to persuade them not to. Listen to the woman talking to her daughters-in-law; the conversation is told at great length. We are meant to listen to it so that we shall begin to understand the extraordinary desolation that now fills the heart of this woman, and empathize with her.

'Go back, my dears,' she says. 'I'm ever so sorry that this has come upon you, but the Lord has acted very bitterly against me. It's no good you following me. We must be realists. I'm old, and I've no more sons.' She's thinking as a Hebrew woman of her time. If only she had had more sons, three or four, then, when the first two died and left their widows, the second two could have been called upon to marry them and continue the family line. 'But I've no more sons,' she says, 'so there's no hope for you young women who are at the threshold of adult life, with all your hopes and expectations now cruelly dashed. It's no good if you're saying you'll wait, because I'm too old to have a husband anyway. And even if I could marry and have children, would you wait these next eighteen years for the boys to grow up? So, thinking of your future and all the longings of your heart, go back, and the Lord grant that each of you may find rest in the house of your new husband' (see 1:8–13).

Emptiness

That phrase 'find rest' is an interesting one: it is the rest of desire, longing and ambition achieved. Nature herself has filled our hearts with longings. And if those longings are forever frustrated or disappointed, except for the grace of God the soul tends to be in torment and turmoil. 'The Lord grant that you may find rest,' Naomi says, 'each of you in the house of your new husband.'

Orpah eventually went back, but Ruth clung to her mother-in-law and followed her back to Bethlehem. As the two women come into the village, the other women see them and exclaim in astonishment, 'This can't be Naomi, can it?'

Why that reaction? Naomi, as she is about to explain, had gone out full; her very name means *pleasantness*. She had obviously come back much changed: gaunt, haunted and sorrowful, in her black widow's garments. And she says, 'Don't call me Naomi; call me Mara, for the Almighty has dealt very bitterly with me. I went away full, and the Lord has brought me home again empty.' A woman in middle life and all her potential now come to nothing; no more prospects, nothing but sorrow and bereavement and gloom. 'Don't call me Naomi,' she says. 'The very name mocks me. Call me Mara [meaning *bitterness*].' And underneath it all, something is fuelling the fires. There's not only bereavement and desolation and hopelessness, but she says, 'The Lord has testified against me' (see vv. 20–21).

It's all right saying that sorrow doesn't come upon us because of our sins; not all the time at any rate. But the godlier a person is, the more they will be inclined when sorrow and frustration like this comes upon them to feel in their conscience: 'Why has the Lord done it? Why has the Lord allowed it? Why does the Lord grant other believers and their families such success?' How difficult it was for Naomi to see young men growing up to serve the Lord and being valiant in Israel, with their proud mothers seeing it all and finding their motherly care fulfilled. 'And my sons are cut off,' she must have thought. 'I have nothing further to live for. The Lord seems to have testified against me,' she says.

The story begins, therefore, with this middle-aged woman, who is desolate, bereaved, broken-hearted and hopeless. 'Can I have sons?' she asks. The story is recorded in all its lovely detail with unexpected twists and delightful surprises (especially if you've not read it before), coming to the climax that we've just read. Naomi's story is the capstone of the book, and at the end, beyond all expectation, she is restored!

Restoration

She had begun to get a little hint of the good things to come when Ruth came back from her first day's gleaning on Boaz's farm. Naomi said to her daughter-in-law, 'May he be blessed by the LORD, whose kindness [or, faithfulness, loyalty] has not forsaken the living or the dead!' (2:20). That terrible engulfing feeling that the Lord has abandoned her begins to recede. 'The Lord has not left off his faithfulness,' she says, as her faith begins to revive again. That's halfway through the book.

At the end of the book her faith is in full flood. For a child is born to Ruth; and you'll notice now that Ruth has virtually disappeared out of the story. Nothing was told of the honeymoon, or those interesting things like what kind of house she lived in. We're simply told that she and Boaz married and a child was born. And the women say to Naomi, 'Blessed be the LORD, who has not left you this day without a redeemer, and may his name be renowned in Israel!' (4:14). And this time they're not talking about Boaz because it goes on to say, 'He shall be to you a restorer of life and a nourisher of your old age, for your daughter-in-law who loves you, who is more to you than seven sons, has given birth to him' (v. 15). We move from Naomi's desolation to Naomi's restoration. 'Then Naomi took the child and laid him on her lap and became his nurse. And the women of the neighbourhood gave him a name, saying, "A son has been born to Naomi." They named him Obed' (vv. 16–17).

We can summarize the story of God's restoration of Naomi in the following table:

Chapter	**GOD'S RESTORATION OF NAOMI**
1	**NAOMI'S DESOLATION**
	» Left of her two sons and of her husband
	» Have I yet sons?
	» Too old for a husband!
4	**NAOMI'S RESTORATION**
	» **Not** left without a kinsman
	» A restorer of life to you
	» Nourisher of your old age
	» A son is born to **NAOMI**

Whatever practical lessons we draw from this lovely little story, we shall not need to wander too far from what is evidently the main subject of the book—the desolation and then the restoration of Naomi. The book isn't about Ruth, as we have said, but the book is rightly entitled 'Ruth' because Ruth is the main figure in the action and is actually the key to Naomi's restoration. Of course, the figure of Boaz is exceedingly prominent and, likewise, a key to Naomi's restoration. But in the end, it will be Ruth who is the key to the action. Let's consider Boaz first.

BOAZ'S SUPPORTING ROLE

The book isn't called 'Boaz', although in one sense the redemption and the restoration depended on him. There were two aspects to this.

Kinsman-redeemer

First of all, Boaz acted as the *kinsman-redeemer* (in Hebrew *go'el*), the near of kin. When Naomi was forced to sell her land by near bankruptcy, Boaz bought the land from her and so kept it in the larger family. And whereas Naomi had not been able to make a go of the farm, Boaz took it over and, with all his resources and wealth, no doubt he made a tremendous success of it.

In Israel in those days, if a man could no longer keep up his farm, he could sell it. But so that the land wouldn't be sold outside the larger family group, it had to be offered to the nearest of kin, and he would buy it, if he could, as a duty to keep the land within the family. Eventually, in the year of Jubilee (which occurred every fifty years), it would revert to the original owner's family (see Lev 25).

If that had been all Boaz did, it would scarcely have satisfied Naomi nor restored her. It would be a bitter thing to admit that she couldn't cope with the inheritance that had been her husband's and her sons', and have to sell it.

Don't ask me how I know, but many of the lords and ladies in the United Kingdom live worried lives, particularly the lords. They've inherited vast estates from their ancestors, going back many hundreds of years. Some have added to their estates and some have lost bits; but it is felt to be an enormous shame to be the one who can't maintain it and has to sell it out of the family. They'll do anything to stop that happening.

In Israel the inheritance was to be maintained and passed down from generation to generation; and to be the generation that lost it would be a disaster. To know that some kinsman had bought it, and therefore it remained in the larger family, would alleviate the suffering a little. But it would do nothing to secure that other thing which was so near to Naomi's heart: the keeping alive of the name of the dead upon his inheritance. If Boaz subsequently sold the land, it would no longer carry the name. In the small villages of those times it was a confession of utter failure and shame for a widow like Naomi to have to sell their farm to somebody else; and for it not to be called Elimelech's farm anymore would advertise to the neighbourhood the failure of Elimelech and his sons.

So it was not enough for Boaz to be the kinsman who bought the land. He could have done that without Ruth, but it wouldn't have satisfied Naomi. Not only did she want to *maintain the inheritance*, she also wanted to *maintain the name* of the dead upon it. For that, Boaz was required to fulfil another institution.

Levirate marriage

In ancient Israel, if a man married and died before he and his wife had a son, as the nearest of kin his brother could be called upon to marry the widow. The first male child born of that marriage would be counted as the son of the first husband and carry on his name.[1] The point of the institution was not merely to keep the deceased man's name upon the inheritance, but the man's name itself from being blotted out as though he had never existed (Deut 25:5–6). Boaz also fulfilled this institution.

You might then say, 'Why didn't Boaz marry Naomi and have a child by her?' Well, for one thing, she was too old. Also, she didn't come into the provision of the law of levirate marriage because her husband had not died childless: he'd had two sons. It was those sons who had died childless, and that was the reason the family name was now in danger of being blotted out completely. It would have been unsuitable, but also impossible, for Naomi to marry Boaz.

So now we can begin to see the importance of the twin institutions upon which the story turns: the kinsman-redeemer and levirate marriage. Only through them can the family name be maintained.

RUTH'S LEADING ROLE

Now we see that the key to the whole situation is not Naomi nor, in that sense, Boaz; it is Ruth. So let's look at that in the structure of the book.

You can see from the contents of the book (overleaf) what the action is and who moves largest in it. Ruth the Gentile becomes key to the restoration of Naomi the Israelite. She was not only brought in for her own benefit. It wasn't

1 This is called levirate marriage from *levir*, the Latin for brother-in-law.

simply that this unfortunate far-off Gentile woman was, by God's grace, brought into the family of God's people and thus blessed; it was far more significant than that. Notice how the proportions of the story therefore concentrate on Ruth and how she came to be that key.

Chapter	**RUTH THE GENTILE: THE KEY TO THE RESTORATION OF NAOMI THE ISRAELITE**
1	Ruth's conversion to faith in Naomi's God and to his people. Her refusal to leave Naomi.
2	Ruth's initiative to go gleaning to support Naomi. Boaz's commendation.
3	Ruth's willingness to marry the 'older' man Boaz. Boaz's commendation.
4	Ruth's child becomes Naomi's child, redeemer and restorer of her old age.

The highlights of chapter 1 are the Gentile Ruth's conversion and profession of faith in Naomi's God, the true and living God; and her determination to cast her lot in with the people of God. The highlight of chapter 2, and the greater part of it, is Ruth's initiative to go gleaning to support Naomi. And notice how Boaz commends her as she meets him in the field on the first day:

> But Boaz answered her, 'All that you have done for your mother-in-law since the death of your husband has been fully told to me, and how you left your father and mother and your native land and came to a people that you did not know before. The LORD repay you for what you have done, and a full reward be given you by

> the LORD, the God of Israel, under whose wings you have come to take refuge!' (vv. 11–12)

In his first commendation of Ruth, Boaz praises her loyalty to Naomi and her family, and her initiative in going gleaning to support Naomi. The key is Ruth, and all the attention is on her in chapter 2.

Chapter 3 is where the romance goes out of the window a little. We need to be careful that we don't read this story in terms of our modern romantic novels. This is an ancient story, and Ruth eventually does what Naomi suggests she should do. When Boaz discovers her and she asks him to marry her (notice where the proposal comes from—I'm told it often does!), Boaz compliments her. Notice what he says:

> May you be blessed by the LORD, my daughter. You have made this last kindness greater than the first in that you have not gone after young men, whether poor or rich. (3:10)

Ruth was a young woman (they would have married very young in those days), and she had married a young man in Moab. And now that she'd come to Israel with all her Moabite charm, she might have married another young man. What struck Boaz was this: 'You have shown more kindness [or, faithfulness, loyalty] at the end than at the beginning. It was marvellous that you came here, following your mother-in-law, instead of going back home to get a husband. You followed her without any prospect of a husband, and when you came you devoted yourself to working hard to maintain her by gleaning in my field. And not only have you maintained her but you've also been prepared to do as she suggests, and seek out an older man [a middle-aged man, most likely] instead of going after the young men' (see 3:10–11).

If Ruth had not been willing to marry such a gentleman, Naomi would never have been restored. We must be careful just now lest we jump too quickly into typology and, drawing from the picture given to us, say, 'Isn't our Lord Jesus Christ lovely, and who wouldn't love him?' Yes, of course, Christ is our great kinsman-redeemer; but at the basic, ground floor level of this story the fact is drawn to our attention that Ruth was prepared to do as Naomi said and ask this middle-aged man to marry her in order to keep the names of Elimelech and Mahlon going, rather than going her own way and marrying a young man and having sons with him.

So Ruth is the key, and when it comes down to the practical application of what this story is saying we shall have to give a great deal of attention to her.

2

APPLICATIONS TO THE PAST AND PRESENT

Readings: Ruth 2:1–20; 3:1–13; 4:17–22

Before you continue, take a little time to read these passages from Ruth. Tap or scan the QR code to read online.

If you're like me, sometimes you might tend to get applications of the Bible a little bit mixed up. I start to apply it at one level, and before I know where I am, I've jumped to another. I'm like a butterfly that hopped on a rose, but then forgot it was after roses and went after dandelions! My butterfly mind makes it extraordinarily difficult for others to follow. So I find it helpful to pause and see that there is more than one level of interpretation and application in Scripture. It will enrich our own personal studies and our preaching and teaching if we can see that there are these different levels in the book of Ruth, and make some effort to keep them moderately distinct.

So first we'll look at the application at the level of what it meant for others in the past, and then what it means now for our salvation in the present. In the next chapter we'll consider some of the practical applications to our own lives of the idea of inheritance. Then in the final chapter we'll think about the book's implications for the future as we consider how it relates to matters of prophecy.

APPLICATION AT THE LEVEL OF HISTORY

If you were expounding this story and wanting to draw lessons from it and apply them for us today, one good place to start would be its historical context. That is given to us at the beginning of the book in the first verse of the first chapter: 'In the days when the judges ruled.' The whole story is set in that historical context, but what is the point of that? Well, look back to the last verse in the book of Judges: 'In those days there was no king in Israel. Everyone did what was right in his own eyes' (21:25). When we come to the end of the book of Ruth, we read that the name of the child born to Ruth is Obed; he was the father of Jesse, the father of David (4:17). There then follows a genealogy, arriving at the great climax of David, the greatest king Israel ever knew, a prototype and ancestor of the Messiah (vv. 18–22). So Ruth has this claim as well, that she became an ancestor not only of David, but of Christ himself.

This means that there is an obvious move in history from a time when there was no king in Israel to the time when David was born. What practical lesson can we learn from this historical detail?

Having a king

First of all, we ought to pause with that phrase about there being no king in Israel and everyone doing what was right in his own eyes. Our natural instinct would perhaps be to say, 'It serves them right for not having a king. It was bound to end up in chaos anyway, with people doing exactly what they liked. Why on earth didn't they have a king?' And then to proceed from that and say, 'Well, mercifully, things got better; eventually they did have a king and his name was David.' But that would be to read it superficially.

In the days of the judges when there was no king, it is the fact that eventually people did what was right in their own eyes. But they didn't start off that way. They didn't have a king because it wasn't God's mind to give them a king at that time. That wasn't an oversight on his part: the reason was that God was king.

You might remember the story of Gideon when he achieved his notable victory and the people wanted to make him king. He said, 'No, I will not be your king. The LORD, your God, is your king' (see Judg 8:22–23). That was true in those early days of Joshua and the elders who outlived him; and it wasn't just a theological doctrine. To those early men, it was a tremendous reality when they gathered the people of God around the tabernacle, believing that God's presence dwelt there. They came together in the awe of the realized and felt presence of God. Then, of course, the kingship of God was a reality to them and worked better than any institution.

What led to the chaos? Israel lost their sense of the reality of the presence and government of God. They still held it as a theological doctrine, but theological doctrines don't work by themselves. If God's rule and kingship is going to have an effect, it has got to be a reality to his people. And the book of Judges tells us how it was that the people lost that sense of the reality of God as king. It was, in part, because the judges broke down. The last one was a horror of a judge. He was doing the very same things from which the first judge had to deliver God's people. But by this time in history, nobody seemed to notice they were wrong. And not only did the judges break down, but the all-tribal assembly broke down. Then the priesthood broke down. In the days of Eli the priest, his sons, Hophni and Phinehas, along with their servants 'treated the offering of the LORD with contempt', and the people lost their sense of his government because of how the priests abused both their position and the people who had come to worship (see 1 Sam 2:12–17).

What was to be the answer? We're told the story in 1 Samuel of how the people got tired of the chaos and came to Samuel and said, 'Look, we're not putting up with this anymore, Samuel. Make us a king like the nations have' (see 8:4–5). Samuel was upset, and God was upset. The people didn't come to God and say, 'Things have gone wrong. Show us where they've gone wrong and what to do about it.' No, they came to God and said, 'We've had it your way for so long; now we're going to have it our way, and that will be better.' Actually, God had intended to give them a king, and he did eventually give them David. But he objected at first because, instead of waiting for him, when the people asked for a king it was a virtual rejection of God.

When he gave them his king, it was a man after his own heart. And eventually from King David, who descended from Ruth and Boaz, came *the* King, Jesus Christ. And the genius was that he is both God and man, so that, in Christ, God is still king! It took many centuries to come about; but to hear these events in a historical context shows the significance of the movement that got Israel from the days when there was no king in Israel and all was moral chaos, to the time of David and eventually to the time of Jesus Christ.

Restoring faith in God's plan

But how was it done? Well, in the historical sense, there was this man called Elimelech. His name in Hebrew means 'my God is king' (*eli* = 'my God', *melech* = 'king'). Some parents today don't take names very seriously. They call their son George, oblivious of the fact that it means 'farmer', and there's probably little likelihood of him growing up to be a farmer. But in the days of the judges, people thought more about what names meant. Very likely, Elimelech's parents were godly people, and in giving this name to their child, they expressed their personal belief: 'My God is king!' Whether he knew it or not, being a Judahite from Bethlehem, Elimelech's father was in the physical line for the coming of *the* King. Listen to Micah:

> But you, O Bethlehem Ephrathah, who are too little to be among the clans of Judah, from you shall come forth for me one who is to be ruler in Israel. (5:2)

Elimelech was in that line and his name was therefore also expressive of the nation's faith. But there came a famine and, fearing that his farm couldn't be worked anymore, he went off to Moab. You mustn't blame him too much, because when there was a famine in the land, Abraham went down to Egypt (Gen 12:10), as did Jacob, with God's permission (46:2–4). When David was rejected by Israel under Saul, he brought his mother and father to the king of Moab and left them in his care until he came to the throne (1 Sam 22:3–4). So we must go easy on Elimelech. But that said, why couldn't the man take these circumstances as from the hand of God, stay put and dare to believe in God's plan and promises? Others did. Obviously Boaz didn't run off, and he and others made a go of it.

We shall never know why Elimelech gave up, but the disastrous result was that he died when he was in Moab, and his sons died there too. That threatened to bring an end to his family line, and the name would perish off the inheritance. Some might have written him off: 'Elimelech didn't amount to much. He came to disaster, his family was wiped out and his widow couldn't make a go of the inheritance. They started off with such confidence that the Lord had given them their inheritance and the Lord was their portion. But it didn't work.' It seemed now to be just theological talk that didn't have any practical merit, and the woman was left hopeless.

What brought Naomi back? In spite of the failure of his people, God himself remained loyal and he brought her back. As we read in Ruth 1, Naomi heard that the Lord had visited his people and there was now grain in Bethlehem, and so she begins to come back. Having arrived there in all the bitterness of her soul, she's now beginning to feel that the Lord has testified against her. But what about this extraordinary Gentile woman called Ruth? Where had her faith come from? The other Gentile woman, Orpah, goes back. Curiously, it is Naomi who advises both of them to go back to Moab and their gods. It seems she couldn't bring herself to believe that Gentiles could get converted. But here's Ruth saying, 'I'll come with you.' Extraordinary! God *could* convert a Gentile—just imagine that. Ruth came to believe in the God of Israel.

As we turn now to chapter 2, we see that when she arrived in Bethlehem Ruth was capable of working, so, rather than waiting for others to maintain her and Naomi, she said, 'Let me go gleaning.' And when she went looking for a field where she might glean, it says, 'She *happened* to come to the part of the field belonging to Boaz [whom she didn't know], who was of the clan of Elimelech' (vv. 2–3). How would you read that? Was it that it just so happened? Or is God in control of our circumstances and even where we work?

If we're going to restore God's people and their belief in the kingship of God in our own personal, practical daily life and its affairs, we shall have to have a sense of the providence of God, and a strong belief in it. You might say it's easy to have that if you are a Boaz with endless bank balances and good health. But when you're in difficult circumstances like Naomi was, it's difficult to believe that the Lord is in it. 'The Lord blessed me,' we say, 'because I got better after an illness, and I got a very good job.' We tend to interpret the Lord's blessing as though it must always be good things. We don't often say, 'I took ill and I lost my job, and the Lord blessed me in that.' But sometimes that is so.

For Naomi, the way back to believing in God began with a glimmer of hope that God was in this. She took it that God had witnessed against her. He had made her bitter and emptied her, in that she went out full and had come back empty. But now when Ruth comes home with the ephah of grain and tells her that the man in whose field she had gleaned was Boaz, and he'd invited her to come back and was kind to her, Naomi sees God's hand in it. She says, 'May he be blessed by the LORD, whose kindness [loyalty] has not forsaken the living or the dead!' (v. 20). God is still loyal, and not only to the present generation; he's loyal to the dead. He'll be loyal to those prayers that have gone up in times past and to the godly longings and aspirations of his people who prayed and have now gone home. God will remain loyal to them.

Naomi is beginning to renew her faith in the providences of God. It was no accident that Ruth got to that particular field and Boaz was showing an extraordinary interest in her; it was of the Lord. It moves Naomi to think, 'If that is of the Lord, I think I can, in faith, now make a suggestion to Boaz.' And so, through Ruth, she did. Boaz accepted, and you know the happy end of the story. Boaz redeemed the land, he and Ruth were married and a son was born to them. And as the women gathered round Naomi, they said, 'Blessed be the LORD, who has given this child to be to you a restorer of life and a nourisher of your old age' (see 4:14–15).

The result of it all was that Naomi was restored and her faith was strengthened. But more than that, she saw there was a future for her, such as she had never dreamed of. Naomi had recovered her sense of the reality of the government and providence of God in her life. And so it is in our lives that the sense of God's providential leading will spur hope and strengthen our testimony for him. But if you're going to maintain a testimony for God, you can't do it without bread and butter, so to speak, to keep you alive. God was working alongside Ruth as she took the initiative to get the food they needed. She went looking for a field where she might glean, and oh, what enormous things turned on that action! The providence of God worked alongside her responsibilities;

and we can still rely upon that providence in all the circumstances of our lives, be they times of sorrow or recovery.

APPLICATION AT THE LEVEL OF SALVATION

There is not merely an application at the historical level of these ancient people, but also at what the theologians would call the soteriological level. That's a magnificent word; it means simply the aspect or way of salvation. The way God brought salvation for Naomi in those far-off days is a prototype of God's way of salvation for us. One of the keys to her restoration is Boaz, the kinsman-redeemer. That idea comes over into the New Testament, for it tells us that the Lord became one of us. He took flesh and blood that he might die and deliver us from fear of death. He is a kinsman-redeemer indeed.

> For he who sanctifies [that is, our Lord Jesus] and those who are sanctified all have one source. That is why he is not ashamed to call them brothers ... Since therefore the children share in flesh and blood, he himself likewise partook of the same things [that is, he became one of us], that through death he might destroy the one who has the power of death, that is, the devil, and deliver all those who through fear of death were subject to lifelong slavery. (Heb 2:11, 14–15)

Boaz was 'a mighty man of wealth' (Ruth 2:1 KJV). But, unlike the nearer kinsman, he had the will as well as the means; not just simply to buy this extra estate, but to buy it and marry Ruth so that their son should inherit it in the name of the other family.

That speaks its message to us at once. As to inheritance, we were strangers from Israel's covenants of promise. But we have our own Gentile inheritance, our heredity, our persons—everything that is summed up in our name, Mary or George or whatever it is. There's not another you in the whole universe. Is there any hope for your unique personality that was given to you by God, but broken by sin? Yes, there is hope, for the Saviour, the Messiah of the Jews, came and preached peace to us who were far off as well as to those who were near (see Eph 2:17).

In Christ we receive an inheritance; and we are made an inheritance. What does that mean? Becoming human, Christ stands with us and has paid the purchase price to redeem us, body, soul and spirit. And not only to redeem us in the sense of forgiving our sins, but one day to redeem our very bodies and change them to become like 'the body of his glory'. Then all the evil results of that sinful heredity will be gone forever and 'we shall be like him' (see Phil 3:21; 1 John 3:2).

There's even more to it than that. There is this matter of maintaining the name. As we've just seen, it wasn't enough for Naomi to sell the land and let Boaz buy it, which would have kept the land in the extended family. Naomi wanted more, and she had a plan. 'My husband and I have been failures, and all the village will know we had to sell up because we couldn't make a go of it.' There was shame in it. But she could see which way the wind was blowing between her daughter-in-law and this wealthy relative and how it would work. So, as we turn to Ruth 3, we see how things begin to develop the night she sent Ruth down to Boaz at the threshing floor. She was to lie at his feet and say to him, 'Spread your wings over your servant, for you are a redeemer' (v. 9). In other words, 'Redeem me.' The Hebrew word for wings (*kānāph*) can also mean the corners of a garment. And we recall that the phrase 'spread your wings' is the same as Boaz himself had used: 'The LORD repay you for what you have done, and a full reward be given you by the LORD, the God of Israel, under whose wings you have come to take refuge!' (2:12). Ruth had come to shelter under the wings of the God of Israel and now she was asking Boaz to spread his wings over her for protection and welcome.

We read in the opening verses of chapter 4 that the next morning Boaz came to the elders at the gate and said to his relative, 'Naomi is selling a piece of land. Would you like to buy it, for you are the nearest of kin?'

He said, 'Yes, I'll buy it.'

So Boaz said, 'You can buy it on one condition, and if you don't fulfil it Naomi won't sell. Are you prepared to marry Ruth in the levirate tradition so that your son will take the name of Elimelech's family? Will you do that?'

And the man said, 'No, I can't. It would mar my own inheritance. Take my right of redemption yourself, for I cannot redeem it' (see vv. 1–6). And, as we know, Boaz was prepared to do it.

What a wise woman Naomi was. She both sold the estate and kept it. It was clever, wasn't it? She sold it out of the family and kept it in the family! In business, where could you sell something and keep it at the same time? But she did. She sold out to Boaz: he bought the land, married Ruth, and their son kept the name of the original family going. What a story at the level of salvation!

Gaining your life

Is there another lesson here for us? Yes, for your inheritance is you! What a 'field' you are, full of potential with your heredity and your name and your abilities. Whatever your name is, it is not just a label; it sums up a whole human being with all that that means. How are you getting on with farming your own particular bit of ground? Are you making a go of it: is it going to last with your name on it for all eternity? Or, being a descendant of Adam, have you not coped as you should with that bit of your inheritance that is yourself, and the weeds have overgrown it?

In fact, that is the verdict of God's law on us, for our handling of the bit of inheritance that is us. We have all personally sinned and come short of the glory of God (see Rom 3:23). We shall never on our own make anything eternal for God out of our inheritance. Is it possible to redeem it?

I once read about pioneers who, in those far-off days, would be paid by the government to clear a portion of forested land for development. It sometimes happened that the entrepreneur, to use the expression, 'bit off more than he could chew' and faced penalties because he couldn't complete the work within the agreed time. To avoid the penalties and get the land developed in time, he would sometimes sell his rights to another entrepreneur.

There was one such man who got converted. He was a rough character, and he came to the Christian man who had led him to the Lord and said, 'I know I'm not supposed to swear, but I can't stop. Not only that, I get the impression that stealing is wrong, and I can't stop that either.'

The Christian man replied, 'Do you really want to stop these things?'

'Yes,' he said, 'but I can't.'

So the Christian man asked him, 'What would you do if you took a part of the forest to clear and couldn't complete it?'

'I'd sell out to someone else,' he said.

'Why don't you sell out your life to Christ?'

It is the only way that your inheritance can be redeemed and your name kept on it, even when you get to heaven. If you sell out your life to him you will keep it, like clever Naomi did. In redeeming it, Christ will let you keep your name on it, though you have become his. 'You are not your own, for you were bought with a price. So glorify God in your body' (1 Cor 6:19–20). Isn't that the secret? And the amazing thing is that Christ will not only let you retain your name, he will develop that name and what it stands for, for his good pleasure to all eternity.

Paul puts it like this, 'For through the law I died to the law, so that I might live to God' (Gal 2:19). There was never a man better than Saul of Tarsus for trying to keep his 'farm' and develop it himself for the glory of God. He thought he had succeeded and was blameless according to the righteousness which is of the law. But the truth caught up with him, and he had to admit that he was a sinner. And he became aware that Jesus was the Son of God and the figure on the cross was the Messiah.

But why did Christ have to die? For all Saul's law keeping, there was no way of saving him other than for Christ to die and pay the penalty of his sin. And so our Lord died, bearing the curse of the law for Saul, who then could say, 'Through the law I died to the law—the law convicted me and I must die.' There was no way of escaping the penalty; but Christ took his place and ours, becoming a curse for us. That is the wonder of it, 'It is no longer I who live, but Christ who lives in me' (Gal 2:20). And yet it is still me, for our Lord does not suppress our individuality or our name.

Our kinsman-redeemer took on flesh and blood so that our name might never be blotted out as though we had never existed. We can reject him and keep our own independence if we like, but it will be an eternal disaster. There will be some whose names will be blotted out of the Book of Life, but selling out to Christ means he will write on us his new name. We are his, but we will keep our inheritance—our heredity and what we are as human beings—and he will maintain and develop it for all eternity. The psalmist said, 'You hold my lot,' (Ps 16:5), and our great kinsman-redeemer will maintain ours.

3

THE IMPORTANCE OF THE INHERITANCE

Reading: Ruth 2:1–17

Before you continue, take a little time to read this passage from Ruth. Tap or scan the QR code to read online.

When **Naomi came back** to her homeland, it was already harvest time. Maybe somebody else had taken the land over, or it had just gone to rack and ruin. There was nothing for them to live on, and how would two women on their own set about ploughing the land and doing the sowing and reaping? It is this inheritance, then, that Naomi decides to sell, with the idea that she can maintain her husband's name on it. The important thing to her was to maintain the inheritance, or to restore it should it have become insolvent and bankrupt. So let's ponder this idea of inheritance, first of all, with Israel and where it started.

ISRAEL'S INHERITANCE

For Israel, the idea of inheritance started when they were redeemed out of Egypt. Having crossed the wilderness, God gave Israel their portion of the land in Canaan as their inheritance. Yes, the original Israelites had to go along with Joshua and fight for it. But then, when the land had been won, Joshua and company solemnly cast lots before the Lord, and where the lot fell each tribe was given their inheritance. Every man got his few acres where he could build his house, wine vat and olive press. There he lived, and there he reared his family. That was his inheritance from the Lord, and as history went by we notice that this attitude to life was very sacred.

There is a story from the time of the kings about how, at one stage, King Ahab decided to take up gardening. He was going to have a beautiful vegetable garden, only it so happened that there was a vineyard belonging to a certain Naboth in the way. So he went along to Naboth and said, 'I want to extend my garden, but your little bit of a vineyard is standing in the way. Now I'll tell you what to do: you'll give me your land, and I'll give you a better vineyard somewhere else. Or if you'd prefer, I'll give you its value in money.'

And to Ahab's astonishment and grief, Naboth said, 'I'm sorry, sir, but no thank you.'

'What do you mean, "No thank you"?'

'Well, no thank you, I don't want to sell my land.'

'I'll give you a good price for it.'

'But you can't buy it: there's no price that I would take for it.'

'Don't be so stupid, man. I'll give you a far better piece of land elsewhere.'

'No land could be better, your majesty. The Lord forbid that I should give you *the inheritance of my fathers.*'

Ahab went off and sulked until Jezebel, who ruled the roost, taught him how to get rid of Naboth and take over the land (1 Kgs 21:1–16).

That story is very interesting in relation to this matter of inheritance. Why wouldn't Naboth sell Ahab his bit of land? It was because Naboth believed that every square inch of dirt and every stone on it was his inheritance from the Lord. It wasn't that he'd been a successful warrior and gained that piece of land, it was because God had given it to his fathers in centuries past. Each generation had maintained it and Naboth wasn't going to give it up. Money couldn't buy it; it was God's inheritance given to him. That made the vineyard itself seem to Naboth a sacred gift from God. But with inheritance comes a tremendous responsibility, both to maintain it in one's own lifetime, and to see it passed down to the next generation.

The Jews had their inheritance, which was given to them when they entered Canaan. As Gentiles, do we have any inheritance, or are we like a lot of stray dogs with no inheritance whatsoever? In the book of Deuteronomy, it says:

> When the Most High gave to the nations their inheritance,
>   when he divided mankind,
> he fixed the borders of the peoples
>   according to the number of the sons of God.
> But the LORD's portion is his people,
>   Jacob his allotted heritage. (32:8–9)

So then Gentiles (the nations) have been given their inheritance, just as God gave the land to the Israelites. But let's leave the nations for the moment and come back to the question of personal inheritance.

PERSONAL INHERITANCE

It would change our attitude to life enormously if we could get round to believing that the same is true of each one of us. My circumstances in life, my home, my job, my abilities—they are a sacred inheritance given by God.

There was a programme I heard on the radio some years ago in which various people were asked, 'If you weren't you, who would you like to be?' It was interesting to hear who people would like to be, and it set me thinking, 'Well, if I weren't me, who would I like to be?' I thought of all the famous names I knew: Charles Spurgeon, David Livingstone and people like that. In the end I decided, no, I would not wish to be any of them, I would like to be myself. That may not be much, but it is by God's grace that I am what I am. And you, my dear fellow believer, may have a far bigger inheritance, but as Paul would put it, changing the metaphor, 'God has set the members, each one of them, in the body just as He pleased' (1 Cor 12:18 NKJV). Money couldn't buy that, could it? *What you are* is an inheritance given to you by God.

A uniquely personal inheritance

What about your circumstances, your piece of ground, your bungalow, your husband or wife, your family—how did you get them? Was it just an accident? Did you manage to carve it out of the jungle? No, surely it's an inheritance that the Lord has given you. Just as Elimelech would have inherited the family ground from his great-great-great-grandfathers, going right back to the time of Joshua, in that sense we have an inheritance as well. Of course, you might have a great estate or something and lots of valuable silver. But whether you have that external stuff or not you've got another inheritance, which in medical terms is called *heredity*.

You are your mother and father, so to speak. And from generations you have a long heredity that governs your physical form, the colour of your eyes, the shape of your nose, your hair, whether you go bald or don't go bald, your good looks or otherwise, and all kinds of things. What do you believe about your heredity? Is it a complete accident, simply a result of Darwin's notions of evolution?

It isn't always an easy question to answer, because along with some of the lovely things that we have inherited from our parents, which we believe are a gift of God, there have come other things, dark things: weaknesses, physical, emotional and mental disabilities. Why am I not somebody else? Why did I have to start off with this particular heredity?

That brings us straight to the whole question of the meaning of life and the matter of inheritance. Is it one ghastly accident, or behind it all is there a God who saw me and surrounded me in my mother's womb (Ps 139:13)? In his providence has he sheltered and guided all my steps?

God the giver

Let's go another step. If you follow Israelite poetry, in the Psalms you'll find that the psalmists have extended the idea of inheritance not simply to the land around them but to all other kinds of benefits. Let's listen to the psalmist in Psalm 16:

The LORD is my chosen portion and my cup;
you hold my lot.
The lines have fallen for me in pleasant places;
indeed, I have a beautiful inheritance. (vv. 5–6)

The psalmist has now spiritualized the idea of inheritance and is no longer thinking of what God has given him by way of cows and grass, honey and milk, a home, a wife and some happy children. He has looked behind the material things to him who is the giver of all the gifts, and he says to himself, 'Ah, I see it. You couldn't measure my inheritance, for I have the giver himself—the Lord is the portion of my inheritance.' And, surveying his inheritance which he has in God, he says, 'The lines have fallen for me in pleasant places.'

He's thinking of the surveyors under Joshua who came along with their measuring lines and laid out the bit of land that was to be given to each man for his inheritance. You can imagine an Israelite waiting there. 'Whose turn is it? Joe's in front of me; I wonder what he's got. Oh, he's got that bit with raised rock in the middle. I'm glad it didn't come out there for me. Mine is this nice, luscious bit of grass. I sympathize with poor Joe, but I'm glad I'm not him. The lines have fallen for me in pleasant places.' But perhaps Joe, who got the piece that was full of hard rock and was disappointed in his lot, was even more ready to see that behind it all was the hand of God the giver. The Levites had nothing; at least, they had no land given to them. God was their portion and their lot (Deut 10:9).

The psalmist says, 'The LORD is my chosen portion and my cup . . . I have set the LORD always before me . . . I shall not be shaken. . . . You will not abandon my soul to Sheol' (Ps 16:5, 8, 10). He's saying that for as long as God exists, he is my portion, and because he is eternal, my portion is eternal, and I shall enjoy it forever.

One other thing was said of Israel. Not only was God their portion, but they were God's portion, and that was in a very special sense. God gave an inheritance to the Gentiles, but as we read in Deuteronomy, he gave a special part to his people, Israel. And not only was the Lord their portion; they were the Lord's portion (32:8–9).

And now in this story of Ruth, we hear how one Israelite found that he couldn't keep up his inheritance from God, and abandoned it. He left his widow virtually bereft and hopeless, with all the shame of it. Then we learn how she came into the good of the redemption, when the inheritance was redeemed and the name of the dead kept upon it. We read of a Gentile who had her inheritance too. It had included a young Hebrew lad as her husband; but he died, and they had no children. Being a Gentile, she wasn't from the nation that was God's portion; she was a stranger to it. The lovely story is how she was brought in and made a part of God's inheritance. Indeed, she was used by God to bring about the restoration of Israel and their inheritance, the whole key to it was this function of a kinsman-redeemer.

CORPORATE INHERITANCE

We come to one more practical application of the story to ourselves. Might it not be that it also has a lesson for us at the level of our history as the people of God in our churches?

The church's history

We have a tremendous inheritance. Now we're not talking about Jewish history but our own Christian history, and yours and mine in particular. There's not only our personal heredity and what we've inherited in our redemption, but what a magnificent inheritance we have among the people of God!

We have the Old Testament Scriptures to start with, and all the benefit of Israel's example. And then there is the New Testament, the distinctly Christian Scriptures. Just think of some of the major movements in our history. When the Scriptures had been lost to people for generations, there came the great Reformation. We owe so much to Martin Luther, John Calvin and others. Then there was the Baptist movement, which recovered the idea of believers being baptized and gathering together as a church, as distinct from a church that is a mixture of believers and unbelievers. You didn't invent that idea, did you? You inherited it. Then there came the Great Evangelical Awakening, with such men as John Wesley and George Whitefield and their emphasis on the need for personal regeneration, not just formal theology. We owe a debt to them every time we sing their delightful hymns. And then there is the principle of the autonomy of each local church in fellowship with others. We inherited it from the apostles, of course, but in more recent history from the Congregationalists who went to America to escape the persecution they suffered for taking their stand on it. What an inheritance we have; not to mention the men and women of more recent times, such as C. H. Mackintosh, J. N. Darby and others.

Now we're here; and what has each of us done with our inheritance? We thank God for those noble men and women who went before us. Have we maintained our inheritance? Or could it sometimes happen that, like Elimelech, we find the theory doesn't work and there comes a famine? The old doctrines somehow begin to lose their grip, we wander and feel there's no future. It could happen, and what shall we do then?

It is here that the book of Ruth comes as a tremendous encouragement to many people. Did the blame lie with Elimelech? Perhaps there's no blame at all, and it was simply one of those things that happened. But when this situation landed on Naomi in her seeming hopelessness and helplessness, with no children to carry on and no hope for the future, she found that God was there. The God who started it all in the early generations with Abraham and Perez and people like that was going to carry it on and bring restoration. And God did restore.

Maintaining the church's inheritance

Praise God, that is the first and it will be the last answer. You don't have to keep a movement going: it's God who brings the revivals and God who will do the restoring. It was God who raised up Gideon and Jephthah. It was God who raised up Luther and Calvin and Whitefield and the rest of them. And what he has done, God can and will do again.

The older you get, and the gap between the generations becomes immense, you'll find this story to be especially full of charm. Who converted Ruth, the key to the restoration of Naomi? God started in a most unlikely place. Here was Naomi saying to her daughters-in-law, 'Things are so far gone that you need to go back to your gods.' What? Can God not convert heathens after all? Can't he do again what he did in the past when he called Abraham out of the sheer idolatry of heathendom? In spite of Naomi's well-meant discouragement, he did it with Ruth. She persisted in her vigorous belief in God. May he do it again in our day and generation, and give us young folks like Ruth.

What a wonderful woman she was. She didn't sit at home with Naomi and say, 'You brought me to this place with all these narrow-minded doctrines, and there's nothing here for me. I don't get anything out of this.' No, she said, 'I'll tell you what, let me go gleaning.' She was devoted to Naomi and to maintaining her, and true conversion means devotion to the people of God. It means loving them and devoting your life to them. It has often and rightly been said that you can't have a public testimony without some spiritual food to keep you alive. We need young men and women who are prepared to say, 'I'll put my back into it for the sake of these curious elderly people of God. I love them because they're Christ's, and I'm prepared to work hard to maintain them.'

Gleaning is hard work—don't read any romance into it. With nose to knees under a burning sun, gleaning would break anybody's back and heart. It was as Ruth gleaned that she first came to the notice of the great Boaz. He didn't let on to start with, but then he began to take her seriously. When did the Lord start to take you seriously?

Boaz began to take Ruth seriously when he saw her among the people of God, gleaning in devotion to her mother-in-law so as to maintain her. He encouraged her to glean only in his field, and at lunchtime he said to her 'Come and eat,' and he gave her some food. Then he told his young men to pull out some bundles for her to glean (see Ruth 2:5–16). He didn't say what some romantic gentlemen would have said: 'Now, Ruth, gleaning is heavy work, so go back home and I'll send round a sack full of grain.' After lunch he let her go back to the hard work.

May God give us more young men and women who are prepared to work hard and save us from the notion that young people can't take rigorous doctrine. They can take physics, they can take computers and many other complicated subjects; surely they can take God's word and glean spiritual food so as to maintain themselves and the people of God.

True conversion means not only devotion to God's people, but also devotion to the Lord Jesus. I know we talk about 'the lovely Lord Jesus', but he doesn't always appear like that to some people. The world has many attractions for the young, but God will reward those who decide that their ambition is to live for Christ.

Ruth made her decision when believing God and being devoted to his people seemed to lead to a dead end in life. It might even have meant remaining unmarried for the rest of her days; but God had other plans, and he honoured her faith. Given the other attractions of younger men, Ruth was prepared to submit to marrying Boaz, an old-fashioned bachelor, for the sake of God's people, and thus to keep the inheritance and maintain the family's name.

What joy there is in living for God and his people. How we could do with that focus again, and the power of Ruth's life experience. To know what it is to lie on the threshing floor overnight, so to speak, and discuss with Christ the wonders that he will do when the morning dawns and the marriage supper of the Lamb takes place. What a joy it is to live for Christ: to experience the wonder of being his bride; to talk to him about his intentions for the redemption and restoration of Israel and the blessing of the world; and by his grace to have a part in it!

4

IMPLICATIONS FOR THE FUTURE

Readings: Ruth 4:9–22; Genesis 38, 42–44

Before you continue, take a little time to read these passages from Ruth and Genesis. Tap or scan the QR code to read online.

Ruth 4

Genesis 38

So far we have had three levels of application. First, at the historical level: to the actual people who lived over three thousand years ago. Then, second, to the institutions through which Naomi was restored: the inheritance and maintaining the name, which give a picture of the great redemption that is in Christ, our kinsman-redeemer. And, third, from these ideas we can glean lessons that apply to us personally and to the church as a whole. Now we come to a fourth level of application as we look at Naomi's story as a prototype of bigger things: the nation of Israel and their restoration.

ISRAEL RESTORED

Though Israel have fallen, God assures us that one day they shall be restored. So that we might begin to take our bearings, let us read some verses in the New Testament that state this explicitly. This is Paul in chapter 11 of his letter to the Romans, talking about the unhappy fact that Israel as a whole have rejected the gospel and their hearts have been hardened. They have stumbled over the stumbling block of Jesus as the Messiah.

> So I ask, did they stumble in order that they might fall? By no means! Rather through their trespass salvation has come to the Gentiles, so as to make Israel jealous. Now if their trespass means riches for the world, and if their failure means riches for the Gentiles, how much more will their full inclusion [Greek, their fullness] mean! (Rom 11:11–12)

It's a lovely truth, isn't it? The fall of Israel, their seeming defeat, their stumbling, their diminution, is not to be permanent. One day their restoration and their fullness will come. And Paul tells us Gentiles not to be high-minded, to imagine that Christ having now come to us Gentiles means that Israel is finished. We are not to be conceited.

> Lest you be wise in your own sight [conceits, KJV], I want you to understand this mystery, brothers: a partial

> hardening has come upon Israel, until the fullness of the Gentiles has come in. And in this way all Israel will be saved, as it is written, 'The Deliverer will come from Zion, he will banish ungodliness from Jacob.' (vv. 25–26)

Once more, Paul is telling us that the hardening of Israel, their stumbling, is only temporary. When the full complement of the Gentiles has come in, then Israel as a whole will be saved. How will she be saved? 'The Deliverer will come from Zion.' A real mighty man of wealth, the kinsman-redeemer, will redeem his people Israel and set them free from all their bondage. These are the plain assured facts from the New Testament.

NAOMI AS A PROTOTYPE

We will find an illustration of that as we look once more to the history of Naomi, to her going into the Gentile land with her husband and coming to distress and despair and almost disaster, when it seemed hopeless that their line would continue. And then the marvellous story of how this Israelite family was eventually restored, and in that process of restoration how the Gentile, Ruth the Moabite, was the key to it all. The story of Ruth and Naomi is a *prototype*. You'll notice I'm not saying a *type*, but rather a prototype. So what do I mean by a prototype?

Take aeroplanes, for example. Some of you, like me, will be old enough to remember those early aeroplanes. When they were so new, if one came over the school (about once in six months) the children used to run out to see it. We were all very proud of this modern invention. They were funny-looking things when you look back on them now: biplanes generally, going 'put-put-put' a few feet above the ground. Today, if you look up at the sky when a big jumbo jet goes over, what a different thing it is from those first humble beginnings. Yet there is a connection between the two.

Those first aeroplanes were what we would call prototypes of the big things that now fly. While there are very great differences between them, there are certain basic similarities. Though the jumbo jet is far more sophisticated and detailed and travels at a far higher altitude, it embodies certain principles of aerodynamics that are the same as those behind the first, humble aeroplanes.

The great God of our redemption has so arranged history that it contains prototypes. Why? So that our minds might be prepared for the coming of Christ; so that we might be sure that Jesus is the Christ and that his salvation does work this way. How can we be sure of that? This same God says, 'Before he comes, I'll give you one or two early examples, some prototypes at a humble level; and if you can see the principle of redemption involved there, you'll be ready to see it when it comes at its highest possible level in the person of Jesus Christ the Lord.'

So the story of Naomi's emptying among the Gentiles, her eventual restoration and fullness, becomes a prototype of bigger things.

Israel as a woman

To help us grasp that, we should notice a very interesting thing in the Old Testament. The prophets frequently talk of Israel or Jerusalem (Zion) as a woman who has been widowed because, it seems to her, God has cut her off. And, notably in the prophecy of Isaiah, she is depicted as a woman bereft of her children:

> Then you will say in your heart:
> 'Who has borne me these?
> I was bereaved and barren,
> exiled and put away,
> but who has brought up these?' (Isa 49:21)

This is not any particular Israelite speaking; it is Israel the nation and Jerusalem the city personified in the form of a woman. When at last the great redeemer comes and brings the children back, she shall say, 'Who has borne me these?' She bewails her predicament, her sorrow and apparent hopelessness, but she is invited to consider that one day there will come forth a redeemer, a true *go'el*, a kinsman-redeemer, and he will redeem Israel and bring her children back again and fill her full. And when he does, it will be like veritable life from the dead. We recall that when he was here on earth, our Lord spoke in a similar way when he said, 'O Jerusalem, Jerusalem . . . How often would I have gathered your children together as a hen gathers her brood under her wings' (Matt 23:37).[1]

Diaspora Jews and the early Christians

The stories in the Acts of the Apostles give us clear examples from the early Christian era to help us see the prototype. If you read very carefully, you will see again and again that Paul went to the synagogue in whatever town he was in, and

1 The idea of wings reminds us of Boaz's words to Ruth in 2:12, and her words to him in 3:9.

he preached there. It was so, for example, when he came to Antioch in Pisidia, Thessalonica, Berea and Corinth (Acts 13, 17, 18). The interesting thing is that these were Jewish synagogues that had been established in Gentile towns.

How did they come to be among the Gentiles? Well, it's a long story that goes back to the days of Nebuchadnezzar, king of Babylon and the earlier Assyrian kings, when God allowed them to take Israel and move her into exile. After that, Alexander the Great took the Jews off into all kinds of Gentile cities, and as they lived there they established their Jewish synagogues in what they called the Diaspora. They were far away from home, living among the Gentiles, but they had their synagogues where they preached the word of God.[2]

As these Jews preached, a lot of Gentiles heard about it and they would come to the Jewish synagogues. We sometimes forget that little bit of history and think that we Christians were the first missionaries to the world. We weren't: the first missionaries to the Gentiles were the Jews. Ever since the exile, they had functioned as missionaries to the Gentiles by preaching the word of God in the synagogues. The Gentiles would come and listen to the rabbis expounding the Old Testament, as it is now known, and preaching the glories of the true God of heaven, as against the miserable, nonsensical darkness of Gentile idolatry. And as they listened, quite a few of them got converted to Judaism.

They had a name for the Gentiles who believed in the living and true God and attached themselves to the synagogues. They called them 'God fearers' or 'God worshippers'. The

2 It happened again from AD 70 onwards, and even more so from AD 133 onwards.

famous Lydia was one like that. We first hear of her when she was at a Jewish prayer meeting by the river in Philippi (Acts 16:13–14). And there were others all over the Roman Empire: men and women who hadn't completely become Jews. They weren't part of the Jewish nation. The men hadn't accepted circumcision, but they used to attend synagogue. They were sort of halfway converts, but they'd come to believe in the living God, just as Ruth had.

Faith in the God of Israel

Naomi and her husband left Bethlehem in Judah. Blame them or don't blame them; they left it anyway, and they went to Moab. Their sons married Gentile women who had been brought up in the crudest of idolatry. It is evident from Ruth 1 that at least one of them had been converted to faith in the God of Israel. Ruth says it quite clearly:

> For where you go I will go, and where you lodge I will lodge. Your people shall be my people, and your God my God. (Ruth 1:16)

Boaz repeats it, for he understands what has happened to Ruth:

> The LORD repay you for what you have done, and a full reward be given you by the LORD, the God of Israel, under whose wings you have come to take refuge! (Ruth 2:12)

She had come to put her faith in the living God, and that is the beginning of conversion. All of us, even in our day and generation, have to take that step if we would be saved. For instance, Paul says of the Thessalonians who were saved that they had 'turned to God from idols to serve the living and true God' (1 Thess 1:9).

Of the large number of those who were converted through Paul's preaching, a high percentage of them were men and women who had already come to faith in the true and living God through the witness of the Jews. What did the Christian preachers tell them beyond that? Well, let's go back to the prototype and the contents of the book of Ruth.

The *NIV Study Bible* has a very helpful outline (see table).

STRUCTURE SHOWING MEANING

The book starts off with Naomi emptied and concludes with Naomi filled. It is very carefully written, and by looking at the end of each of the major movements, we can see there is a theme of 'Ruth returning' that runs through it. Ruth and Naomi *return* to Bethlehem at the end of chapter 1. Ruth *returns* to Naomi at the end of chapter 2. Ruth *returns* to Naomi at the end of chapter 3. And then, of course, Ruth is married, and her child is born and put on Naomi's lap in chapter 4.

Ruth, way down in Moab, had come to believe in Israel's God, the living and true God; and in chapter 1, she is proud to take her stand with the people of God and leave her heathen family and country. Listen again to the wonderful story. Naomi and Ruth start the journey back. Naomi is still feeling absolutely empty, her future bleak, the name of her husband and sons lost forever, or so she thinks. She feels that the Lord is angry with her and has testified against her, and there's no hope for her and her family. But Ruth sticks to her, and so eventually they get home.

Book of Ruth: Table of Contents

Chapter			
1	1:1–5	Introduction: *Naomi emptied*	
	1:6–22	Naomi returns from Moab	
		A. 1:6–18	Ruth clings to Naomi
		B. 1:19–22	Ruth and Naomi return to Bethlehem
2	Ruth and Boaz meet in the harvest fields		
		A. 2:1–7	Ruth begins work
		B. 2:8–16	Boaz shows kindness to Ruth
		C. 2:17–23	Ruth returns to Naomi
3	Ruth goes to Boaz at the threshing floor		
		A. 3:1–5	Naomi instructs Ruth
		B. 3:6–15	Boaz pledges to secure redemption
		C. 3:16–18	Ruth returns to Naomi
4	4:1–12	Boaz arranges to marry Ruth	
		A. 4:1–8	Boaz confronts the unnamed kinsman
		B. 4:9–12	Boaz buys Naomi's property and announces his marriage to Ruth
	4:13–17	Conclusion: *Naomi filled*	
	4:18–22	Epilogue: Genealogy of David	

Adapted from Kenneth L. Barker (gen. ed.)
NIV Study Bible, Grand Rapids, Michigan: Zondervan, 2002.

Then comes chapter 2. It wasn't Naomi who said to Ruth, 'I have a relative who's very rich and has got a big farm. You should go and glean with him.' The historian tells us that there was such a man around the place, but Naomi didn't advise Ruth to go and seek him. It was Ruth who discovered him. She said to Naomi one bright morning, 'I'd like to go gleaning in a field somewhere. I don't know where, but perhaps I could find grace in the eyes of one of the local farmers and get some grain to feed us. We desperately need it.' So Naomi said, 'You go, my dear.'

Meeting a gracious man

Ruth went and gleaned in a field, but she didn't know whose field it was. When the farmer came along, his name was Boaz, and he was a very rich man. To her surprise, he was kind to her. He asked his foreman who she was, and the foreman said, 'She is the Moabite woman who came back with Naomi, and she's been gleaning hard all day long.' So he went to talk to her, and, of course, she was nervous. 'I want you to stay in my field', he said, and Ruth was so overwhelmed she fell on her face and bowed herself to the ground and said, 'Why have I found favour in your eyes, that you should take notice of me, since I am a foreigner?' (see Ruth 2:8–10).

It wasn't everybody who would have welcomed the woman, not even in Bethlehem. They should have done so. The law said that at harvest time the farmer was to leave the gleanings in the field for the poor and the foreigner (Lev 19:9–10). That's what the law said, but businessmen don't always keep to the law if they can make extra money. Not everybody would have welcomed this foreigner from Moab taking their grain. In addition, Boaz said to Ruth, 'You should keep close to my young women, and I've told my young men not to harm you' (see Ruth 2:8–9). In those dark days it could have been a very dangerous thing for Ruth to have gone to another field amongst other rough men at a time of harvest. And then, to her overwhelming sense of wonder, he invites her to sit with him and the workmen and eat a meal with them. Then he personally hands her some food. She was absolutely flabbergasted by the grace of this gentleman farmer, who would take such an attitude to a foreigner. He said, 'I know you're a stranger, but it's been fully shown to me what your attitude to your mother-in-law has been since your husband died. And that you've come to believe and to take refuge under the wings of the living God' (see vv. 11–15).

Ruth tells Naomi

Can you hear the buzz of conversation when she returned home that night? Ruth and Naomi have a real chinwag about the events of the day. Here comes Ruth with this grain that she's gathered and threshed. It was an unusually large amount because Boaz had ordered the workmen to drop handfuls on purpose. They left great big armfuls of the stuff for her. She's got a whole ephah[3] of grain, and she says to Naomi, 'There's not only what I gleaned, but at lunchtime he personally handed me a lot of food. I ate until I was full and here's what I had left over.' That was a great heap as well. Oh, the wealth and the grace of it! You can imagine their joy as the young woman told her mother-in-law about discovering this man of grace in Bethlehem-Judah.

It wasn't Naomi who had directed Ruth. Naomi had directed her to the one true God, but Ruth the Gentile

3 An ephah was about ⅗ bushel or 22 litres.

had found something else within Israel. She had found this extraordinary man of grace who had welcomed her, knowing that she was a Gentile from despised Moab, with its dark and immoral past. When Naomi heard that, you know it was like a little snowdrop bulb, deep in the earth under the cold of winter, suddenly hearing the call of spring, and life begins to stir. She said, 'You know, Ruth, he's one of our kinsmen, a *go'el*.' In the very word there was all sorts of potential; and just think it was the Gentile who discovered him first!

As the conversation continued, we read 'Ruth the Moabite [it's pointing out the fact that she was a foreigner] said, "Besides, he said to me, 'You shall keep close by my young men until they have finished all my harvest.'" And Naomi said to Ruth, her daughter-in-law, "It is good, my daughter, that you go out with his young women"' (2:21–22). Amongst all the farmworkers, it was perhaps only Boaz's young men who could be trusted, and only his young women who would have welcomed her. To be practical, if many of those young women were unmarried and the number of eligible gentlemen was rather restricted, they may not have welcomed the competition and Ruth might have had a rough time coming in as a foreigner. But she found a welcome among the workers in Boaz's field because they were the men and women of Boaz. Ruth was so excited as she came home to her mother-in-law to tell this Jewess about what she had discovered in Israel.

Just think again about Paul coming to those synagogues and telling the Gentiles who had believed in the true and living God about the mighty man of grace and wealth from the royal stock of Bethlehem, who at his birth was laid in a manger. What a story they heard, and how great was their discovery of the Messiah of God. Whereas Judaism tended to be very severe and keep strangers at arm's length, here was a saviour who was prepared to welcome them, Gentiles though they were. They could even be saved without being circumcised and becoming members of the Jewish nation. There must have been many a conversation in those ancient cities in the early days of Christianity, as the Gentiles told those yet unconverted Jews what they had discovered. And as they listened, just as many centuries before the Israelite Naomi listened to the Gentile Ruth, their hearts must have been stirred as they remembered God's ancient promises about the great redeemer who was to come.

Grace restores

Eventually Naomi told Ruth to go down to the threshing floor and make her request to Boaz. So down the Gentile woman went, and she said to this very approachable and gracious man, 'You are a kinsman; would you redeem me?' And he said, 'Yes, I will. Tomorrow I'll do all that is required. There is a nearer kinsman who has first rights, but so long as he's not willing to redeem you and he passes on the rights to me, then I will redeem you and I will marry you' (see 3:1–13).

And Ruth went home. 'How did you get on, my dear?' said Naomi, almost breathless, as Ruth came through the door, staggering under six whole measures of grain. I suspect it was as much as the sturdiest of young women could carry. For Boaz had said, 'Bring your shawl here, and let me put some barley into it. You mustn't go home to your mother-in-law *empty*' (see 3:15–17).

How God makes us eat our words sometimes! This was the woman who came back to Bethlehem and said to her neighbours, 'I went out full and the Lord has been hard against me, and he's brought me home *empty*. There's no future for me.' Now here comes Ruth, staggering under this gift: 'Boaz said I wasn't to come home to you *empty*.' What a testimony, and what a gospel messageto preach to this woman of Israel! She said to Naomi, 'Tomorrow he will redeem the inheritance and he will marry me.' So that was good news indeed!

We go back again to the early Christians testifying to the Jews. Not only did they come to believe in the true and living God; they heard the story of grace and discovered Jesus, born in Bethlehem, who welcomed even Gentiles. Next, they heard the almost incredible message that this great redeemer-saviour loved the church, which was being formed not only of Jews but also of Gentiles. He loved it as a man loves his wife; and when his redemption is complete there will be the marriage of the Lamb and Gentiles will be part of that bride (Eph 5:25; Rev 19:7–9). When the first Christians told it to their Jewish friends, this was a new kind of talk. The Jews knew about God as the husband of Israel (Isa 54:5), but they never dreamed that the Messiah would have a wife.

Isn't this what Ruth was saying? She'd found Boaz, the great kinsman-redeemer, who was not only able to feed and satisfy her soul and fill her heart with the treasures of his grace, but he had a proposal of ultimate marriage for her. Don't you wish you had a magic carpet to take you back to that home as Ruth and Naomi talked over what was going to happen tomorrow? Did they go to bed at all? Could they take it in? Naomi's great kinsman was not going to marry her, of course, but rather Ruth. And so he did!

Do you make a habit of witnessing to Jews, if you get the chance? I once had a dear Jewish friend, who found it difficult to think of Jesus as the Messiah. He thought of Christians as people who had learned to persecute Jews and were responsible for all the anti-Semitism that resulted in six million being gassed and destroyed by Hitler. He would say to me, 'You Christians are responsible for it. You told the world and taught the children in Sunday school that it was the wicked Jews who crucified Jesus. You stirred up hatred in their hearts, and the result was that six million of my people were murdered. How can Jesus be the Messiah?'

I would say to my friend, 'I know you don't think much of Jesus, but I want to tell you something about him. He is the one Jew beyond all others who has led millions of Gentiles to believe in the God of Israel. I don't believe in just any old god; I believe in your God, the God of Abraham, Isaac and Jacob. And if you want to know how I came to do that, it was because of Jesus. It was an evil thing beyond description that Hitler did, but what Jesus Christ has taught me is to love Jews.'

What a marvellous testimony it was as Ruth the Gentile talked to Naomi the Jewess. And what a thing it shall be for Israel when *the* kinsman-redeemer will acknowledge his bride and take her to be his wife, not merely at the gate of some little village in Judaea, but at the resplendent gates of heaven and before the whole universe.

The final fulfilment of the prototype

When the full complement of the Gentiles has been brought in, what then? Well, Israel shall come into her fullness. So did Naomi, of course. The result of it all was not only that Naomi's faith was restored and strengthened, but she now saw there was a future for her such as she had scarcely dreamed of. The baby that Naomi now laid on her lap would be a restorer of life and a nourisher of her in old age—he would be her redeemer.

When the Gentiles have fully come in, all Israel shall be saved. If their setting aside, their diminution, their fall proved to be the riches of the Gentiles, the receiving of them again will be like veritable life from the dead (see Rom 11:15); just as Naomi's wandering to Moab proved to be Ruth's immeasurable riches and her own glorious restoration.

We read in Ruth 4 that at the official wedding, when Boaz claimed Ruth as his bride, all the well-wishers stood around and said some pleasant things, as people do at weddings. Sometimes they say funny things they wouldn't say on any other occasion, if they respected their intelligence! But these weren't funny things. They said, in the first place, 'May the LORD make the woman, who is coming into your house, like Rachel and Leah, who together built up the house of Israel. May you act worthily in Ephrathah and be renowned in Bethlehem' (4:11). That was a very nice wish. They were comparing Ruth to Rachel and Leah—a wise thing, for Rachel and Leah began life as Gentiles too. They were married to Jacob, and these erstwhile Gentiles (with their handmaids' help) built up all twelve tribes of the house of Israel.

We can understand that much, but then they added a curious thing: 'And may your house be like the house of Perez, whom Tamar bore to Judah, because of the offspring that the LORD will give you by this young woman' (v. 12). What on earth did they mean? If you've read the story recently, you'll wonder why anybody dared to mention it at a wedding. Surely such history ought to have a veil drawn over it, and it's not a chapter that's normally read publicly in Christian churches. Can you remember when you last heard it read, if ever? And yet, like all of God's word, it is profitable.

The story of Tamar and Judah

The story of Tamar, who bore Perez to Judah, is given in Genesis 38. But whatever has it got to do with Ruth and her situation? Well, two obvious similarities are at once apparent. First, in both stories we're dealing with someone from Judah. Elimelech came from Judah, from Bethlehem indeed. Secondly, both stories involve the royal line of Judah. Look at the genealogy at the end of Ruth 4. There Perez is mentioned, and his significance is that, of all the sons of Judah, Perez was the one who led the royal line of Judah until it came to King David himself. And in that royal line was Boaz, who married Ruth. So Judah and Tamar produced Perez, and eventually in the same line came Boaz and Ruth, Obed, Jesse and then King David.

Tamar was a Gentile, so you will see the connection. More than that, both stories talk about the institution of levirate marriage. But the particular point to note at this moment is that, just as in the book of Ruth it was a Gentile who was the key to the maintenance of the line that led to the king, so in this far-off story in Genesis 38 it was the Gentile woman, Tamar, who was concerned to maintain the line of the king, when, through Judah's folly and irresponsibility, the line would have petered out before it started.

Perhaps Judah didn't know it at the time, but he was destined to be the founder of that line which should lead not only to King David but to the Lion of the tribe of Judah himself. Perhaps it was his ignorance of this that accounted for his strange behaviour. But after the brothers had rejected

Joseph and sold him to the Gentiles then Judah went down from them to the Gentiles as well. So Joseph was among the Gentiles, and Judah was among the Gentiles. Judah didn't have much notion of his duty to raise up the line of the king, so what good was he to the Gentiles? He married a Gentile woman and had two sons by her, and then a third. The two sons were eventually married to Tamar, another Gentile woman. The first son was married to her and died without children. So Judah, following levirate law, married the second son to her, but he also died without children. The third son was very much younger, so Judah said to Tamar, 'Go back to your father's house and wait until my third son is grown up' (see v. 11). But when the boy had grown up, Judah made no attempt to give him to Tamar to be married. He was afraid that this son would die too.

At that point, a very curious thing happened. See Judah one fine day after he'd been to the sheep shearers, and I dare say he had made a lot of money. And, of course, he was head of the tribe, with his staff of office and signet ring. You weren't anybody if you didn't have a signet ring with your emblem on it to sign your name with. It was tied with a beautiful cord around Judah's neck.

So he was going downtown. His work was over and he'd got the money, so why shouldn't he have a good time? That's what life is for, isn't it? He met a woman whom he thought was a prostitute and promised to pay her. She wanted a pledge, and he asked her what he should give her, and she said, 'Your signet and your cord and your staff that is in your hand' (see vv. 16–18). So he gave them to her. Afterwards, not wanting to be seen in the area, he sent his friend to redeem the pledge. But the woman wasn't there, and so the signet on the cord and the staff of office went missing.

When, some months later, it was announced that his daughter-in-law was going to have a child through an immoral relationship, Judah commanded that the woman be executed. 'I won't have that kind of thing going on in my family,' he said. Hypocrite. And just as they were going to execute the woman, she sent Judah the evidence of his staff and his signet. 'You judge the man they belong to,' she said, 'he's the father of my child' (see vv. 24–25).

I suspect you disapprove of what Tamar did, but her aim was to maintain Judah's line even though she was a Gentile. She was more concerned to maintain the line of Judah than he was himself. Do we have a little prophecy there? Particularly in the Christian era, Gentiles have been more concerned about the line of Judah and the coming King-Messiah than Jews have. While some Orthodox Jews still believe in the coming of the Messiah, most Jews, even those who go to their synagogues, don't believe in it anymore. The greatest interest in the coming of the Messiah is to be found among Gentiles.

The responsibility of being linked to the king

One last thing. As we have seen, Tamar and Ruth were used by God to maintain the royal line that would eventually lead not only to King David but to the Lion of the tribe of Judah himself. But what does it mean to be in the line of the king? Well, Judah had very dim notions of the future that lay beyond being head of his tribe. What do you suppose he thought it was all about? Was being head of the tribe just about enjoying yourself and being the big man? That is the concept of kingship for many folks, and indeed it was so even with the apostles.

There was one occasion when our Lord was going up to Jerusalem to suffer at Calvary, and Mrs Zebedee came up to him with her sons. She said, 'We've got a request to make. Please grant that my two sons sit, one at your right hand and one at your left in your kingdom.'

And the Lord Jesus said to her, 'Are you aware of the cost of such a thing? Can you be baptized with the baptism I'm baptized with? And drink the cup I drink?'

'Oh yes,' they said, 'we don't care what it costs. We want the chief jobs.'

Said the Lord Jesus, 'That isn't mine to give anyway; that's decided by my Father. But do you have any idea what it means to be king, and what it means to have the chief jobs in the kingdom? What do you think it means?'

'Oh, we think it means sitting on thrones and bossing people around.'

'It doesn't mean that. I am the King myself. And the Son of Man came not to be served but to serve, and to give his life as a ransom for many' (see Matt 20:20–28; Mark 10:35–45).

That's what it means to be in the line of the king, and what Judah had to learn. For there is another story about Judah, but he's a very different man now. Not now a Judah who thinks that being the head of the tribe is an excuse for just enjoying yourself irresponsibly, caring little about the survival of the line of the king. The story in Genesis 42 onwards is about how Joseph's brothers came down to Egypt to buy grain when there was a famine in Canaan. When they came the second time, the condition was that they should bring their youngest brother, Benjamin, with them. At first

Jacob wouldn't let Benjamin go. He said, 'I've lost Joseph, I've lost Simeon. Now if you take Benjamin and some ill happens to him, it will bring me down to the grave. You mustn't take Benjamin.'

Judah said, 'But the man said we must, and if you don't let Benjamin go, we can't go back. We shall not get grain unless we bring Benjamin. You'll have to let him go.'

Reuben volunteered to be responsible for him. 'Don't talk nonsense, Reuben,' said Jacob. 'I know about you.'[4]

So Judah stepped forward and said, 'I'll be responsible for him, and I'll see no harm comes to him.'

And on that condition, Jacob let Benjamin go.

They went down to Egypt, and you know what happened. When they were on their way back home, they were overtaken by Joseph's steward, who said, 'One of you has stolen my lord's cup.' The cup was found in Benjamin's sack, and they all went back to Egypt in tremendous distress. And Joseph said, 'All the rest of you can go back home, but you agreed that the man in whose sack the cup was found would have to stay behind.'

At that moment, Judah stepped forward and said, 'Sir, my father is old, and this is his last son. He dotes on him, and his whole life is bound up with this lad. He didn't want him to come. He said, "If he goes and he's lost, it will kill me." I went as guarantor for him, and if I go back and Benjamin is not with me, it will bring my father down to the grave brokenhearted. I can't go back and see what that would do to him. Please, would you let me take the place of Benjamin and suffer his penalty for him?'

4 See Gen 35:22; 49:3–4.

Through Joseph and his wisdom, Judah had been taught a lesson. What does it mean to be in the line of the king? It doesn't mean going down the street with your staff, commanding everybody and carelessly indulging yourself. Whether he knew it or not, Judah was beginning to act like one in the line of the king who would come to give his life as a ransom for many.

THE PAST POINTING FORWARD

We come back finally to Ruth, that marvellous woman. Hers is the story of a Gentile who came to faith in God, discovered the great kinsman-redeemer and laid down her life for the people of God. She had decided to go with Naomi when, humanly speaking, that would mean the end of all her hopes. She was prepared to give her life for that nation. And John the apostle says, 'By this we know love, that he laid down his life for us, and we ought to lay down our lives for the brothers' (1 John 3:16).

While Israel wandered from God, there were Gentiles who came to believe not just in any god, but in the God of Abraham, Isaac and Jacob. There's a conversion for you! Still to this day, Gentiles come in their thousands and millions to believe in the God of Israel. And true conversion makes Christians devoted to the maintenance of Israel's place in God's plans. Alas for those misguided notions that hold that the church has replaced Israel and Israel has gone forever. That is not true and has been the source of much scandal.

Israel's wandering—their exile and rejection of their Messiah—has brought salvation and riches to the Gentiles (see Rom 11:12). We Gentiles have come to know the Jew,

Jesus, as our Messiah, our kinsman-redeemer. When he comes and publicly acknowledges us and completes the redemption of our bodies, and when the marriage supper of the Lamb takes place, it shall lead to the restoration of Israel in her old age.

That is the story of how a Gentile maintained the line of the king. And if we ourselves would be effective witnesses, like Ruth was to Naomi the Israelite, and used by God in the great processes that one day shall see Jesus Christ come in all his glory, then we must be prepared to follow the king and lay down our lives for all of God's people, both Jews and Gentiles.

These are not fairy stories. We are to believe that what happened in Ruth's day and has happened in many a generation since, God could do still in our day and generation. He will maintain the name of the coming Messiah upon his inheritance. When the Lord Jesus comes, Israel will be vindicated. It will be Israel's God who is proved to be the true God, and Jesus the Jew whose name will be acknowledged as *The Lion of the tribe of Judah* (Rev 5:5).

MYRTLEFIELD HOUSE WEBSITE

Our website contains hundreds of resources in a variety of formats. You can read, listen to or watch David Gooding's teaching on over 35 Bible books and 14 topics. Our website is optimized for both computer and mobile viewing, making it easy for you to access the resources at home or on the go.

For more information about any of our publications or resources contact us at: info@myrtlefieldhouse.com

MYRTLEFIELD EXPOSITIONS

Myrtlefield Expositions provide insights into the thought flow and meaning of the biblical writings, motivated by devotion to the Lord who reveals himself in the Scriptures. Scholarly, engaging and accessible, each book addresses the reader's mind and heart to increase faith in God and to encourage obedience to his word. Teachers, preachers and all students of the Bible will find the approach to Scripture adopted in these volumes both instructive and enriching.

The Riches of Divine Wisdom
The New Testament's Use of the Old Testament

According to Luke
The Third Gospel's Ordered Historical Narrative

True to the Faith
The Acts of the Apostles: Defining and Defending the Gospel

In the School of Christ
Lessons on Holiness in John 13–17

An Unshakeable Kingdom
The Letter to the Hebrews for Today

MYRTLEFIELD ENCOUNTERS

by David Gooding and John Lennox

Myrtlefield Encounters are complementary studies of biblical literature, Christian teaching and apologetics. The books in this series engage the minds of believers and sceptics. They show how God has spoken in the Bible to address the realities of life and its questions, problems, beauty and potential.

Key Bible Concepts
Defining the Basic Terms of the Christian Faith

Christianity: Opium or Truth?
Answering Thoughtful Objections to the Christian Faith

The Definition of Christianity
Exploring the Original Meaning of the Christian Faith

The Bible and Ethics
Finding the Moral Foundations of the Christian Faith

MYRTLEFIELD DISCOVERIES

Myrtlefield Discoveries combine depth of insight with accessible style in order to help today's readers find the Bible's meaning and its significance for all of life. Covering whole books of the Bible, themes or topics, each book in this series serves as a guide to the wonders of God's word. The material is intended to prepare readers to share what they have learned. Study groups, teachers and individual students will all benefit from the way these books open up the biblical text and reveal its application for life.

Drawing Near To God
Lessons From the Tabernacle for Today

Windows on Paradise
Scenes of Hope and Salvation in the Gospel of Luke

Journeys with Jesus
True Stories of Changed Destinies in John's Gospel

MYRTLEFIELD DEVOTIONALS

The first of these 365 one-page readings focuses on the work of Christ as the one who brings us through life's journey to the destination of being like him.

The second volume aims to deepen our understanding of some of the characteristics of our God in the assured hope that such understanding will renew our minds and, consequently, the way we live our lives.

Bringing us to Glory
Daily Readings for the Christian Journey

Changing us for Glory
Daily Readings on God's Transforming Power

Also available.

The Letters of David W. Gooding
Answering Questions Related to the Christian Faith

THE QUEST FOR REALITY AND SIGNIFICANCE

A Six Part Series
by David Gooding and John Lennox

We need a coherent picture of our world. Life's realities won't let us ignore its fundamental questions, but with so many opposing views how will we choose answers that are reliable? In this series of books, David Gooding and John Lennox offer a fair analysis of religious and philosophical attempts to find the truth about the world and our place in it. By listening to the Bible alongside other leading voices, they show that it is not only answering life's biggest questions—it is asking better questions than we ever thought to ask.

1. Being Truly Human: *The Limits of Our Worth, Power, Freedom and Destiny*

This addresses issues surrounding the value of humans. It considers the nature and basis of morality, compares what morality means in different systems, and assesses the dangerous way freedom is often devalued. What should guide our use of power? What should limit our choices? And to what extent can our choices keep us from fulfilling our potential?

2. Finding Ultimate Reality: *In Search of the Best Answers to the Biggest Questions*

The authority behind ethics cannot be separated from the truth about ultimate reality. Is there a Creator who stands behind his moral law? Are we the product of amoral forces, left to create moral consensus? Gooding and Lennox compare ultimate reality as understood in: Indian Pantheistic Monism, Greek Philosophy and Mysticism, Naturalism and Atheism, and Christian Theism.

3. Questioning Our Knowledge: *Can We Know What We Need to Know?*

How can we know whether any of the competing worldviews are true? What is truth anyway, and is it absolute? How would we recognize truth if we encountered it? Beneath these questions lies another that affects science, philosophy, ethics, literature and our everyday lives: how do we know anything at all?

4. Doing What's Right: *Whose System of Ethics is Good Enough?*

Particular ethical theories claim to hold the basic principles everyone should follow. Gooding and Lennox compare the insights and potential weaknesses of each system by asking: what is its authority, its supreme goal, its specific rules and its guidance for daily life? They then evaluate why even the best theories prove to be impossible to follow consistently.

5. Claiming to Answer: *How One Person Became the Response to Our Deepest Questions*

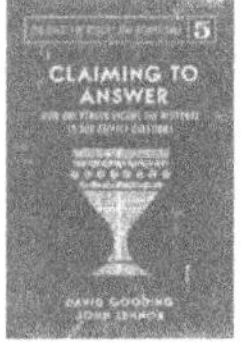

It is not enough to have an ethical theory telling us what standards we ought to live by, because we often fail in our duties and do what we know is wrong. How can we overcome this universal weakness? Many religions claim to be able to help, but is the hope they offer true? Gooding and Lennox state why they think the claims of Jesus Christ are valid and the help he offers is real.

6. Suffering Life's Pain: *Facing the Problems of Moral and Natural Evil*

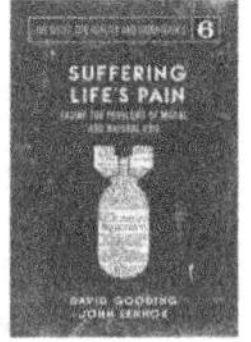

There is a problem with believing in a wise, loving and just God who does not stop natural disasters or human cruelty. Why does he permit congenital diseases, human trafficking and genocide? Is he unable to do anything? Or does he not care? Gooding and Lennox offer answers based on the Creator's purpose for the human race, and his entry into his own creation.

ABOUT THE AUTHOR

Photo credit: Paul Watson

David W. Gooding (1925–2019) was Professor of Old Testament Greek at Queen's University Belfast and a Member of the Royal Irish Academy. He taught the Bible internationally and lectured on both its authenticity and its relevance to philosophy, world religions and daily life. He published scholarly articles on the Septuagint and Old Testament narratives, as well as expositions of Luke, John, Acts, Hebrews, the New Testament's Use of the Old Testament, and several books addressing arguments against the Bible and the Christian faith. His analysis of the Bible and our world continues to shape the thinking of scholars, teachers and students alike.

www.ingramcontent.com/pod-product-compliance
Lightning Source LLC
LaVergne TN
LVHW050609100826
845148LV00015B/3189

9781836760689